£3

GLASGOW

SOME CITY

ROBIN WARD

GLASGOW

SOME CITY

ROBIN WARD

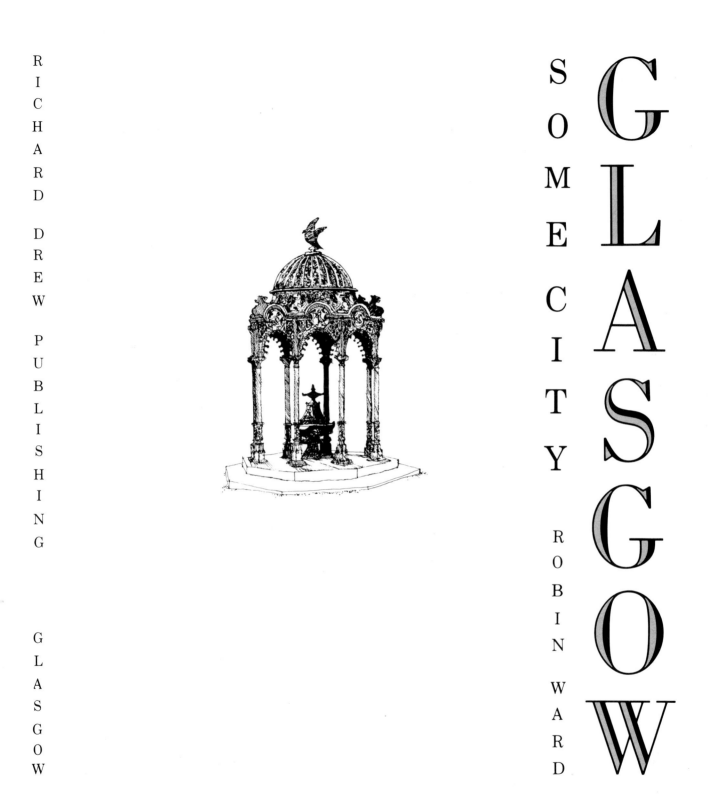

RICHARD DREW PUBLISHING

GLASGOW

For My Parents

Above: The Iron Building, Jamaica Street
Title page: Cast-iron fountain, Glasgow Green
Cover: Kelvingrove Museum and Art Gallery

Richard Drew Publishing Limited
6 Clairmont Gardens
Glasgow G3 7LW
Scotland

First Published 1982
Reprinted 1982
Revised Edition 1988
© Robin Ward 1982, 1988
ISBN 0 86267 205 8

Designed by Robin Ward
Photoset in Century Schoolbook by Swains (Glasgow) Limited
Printed and bound in Great Britain by Butler & Tanner Ltd, Frome and London

CONTENTS

I This book is an evocation of Glasgow with particular reference to the city's 19th-century
N architecture illustrating the astonishing variety of Victorian buildings in Glasgow and
the often improbable cross-cultural connections which contribute to its character. There
is a Venetian palace on Glasgow Green, there are Parisian and Art Nouveau tenements,
T Chicago style commercial buildings, Gothic and Greek churches, Scottish baronial style
banks and Egyptianesque warehouses.

R Glasgow in its heyday was the Second City of the British Empire, a vast, smoky met-
ropolis founded on the 18th-century American tobacco trade and 19th-century manu-
O facturing and engineering — textiles, shipbuilding, steam locomotives, iron, coal and
chemicals. Between 1870 and 1914, for example, Clyde shipyards alone produced 18 per
D cent of the world's steamships. At their peak, just before the First World War, this was
closer to one-third. By the 1890s Glasgow's Springburn area was building more steam
U locomotives than any other centre in Europe. A staggering 71 per cent were for export,
mainly to the colonies.

C The city had its share of squalor and slums but it also had a flourishing *fin-de-siècle*
cultural and artistic life surfing on the wave of its industrial success. Yet for all its parks
T and art galleries it had little of the polished, civilised veneer of, say, Paris, Vienna or
Edinburgh. Glasgow was primarily an industrial, not a capital city. It was the Hamburg
I or Chicago of Scotland. What it did have was its architecture. This was the medium in
which the city's industrial and mercantile moguls chose to express and represent them-
O selves — and how they built. Glasgow above the shopfronts is a mighty city of grand com-
mercial and civic façades. Its 19th-century commercial, civic and industrial buildings,
N tenements and terraces achieve a level of architectural distinction unequalled elsewhere
in Britain. They form a Victorian townscape of incomparable concentration and variety.

The city which the Victorians built in the hectic imperial Klondike between 1850
and 1900 was, architecturally, one of the finest of its era in the world — a Victorian city
par excellence. This was not always appreciated as it is today. In the 1960s, Glasgow's

19th-century buildings seemed to those in power to be symbols of the city's decline rather than its past pre-eminence or, indeed, potential renaissance. The city found it difficult to come to terms with its calamitous decline and to understand that the singular circumstances which made it the 'workshop of the British Empire' would never be repeated. Glasgow's politicians spoke with a Victorian confidence and ambition while the heavy industry to back them was closing down. Even shipbuilding, which for so long sustained the city's reputation, is now only a reflection of its former self. The majestic forest of cranes which bestrode 20 miles of riverbank has been pulled away leaving only solitary clumps of this ennobling activity. 'We don't just build ships here,' a Govan shop steward once remarked, 'we build men.' Not anymore. The docks and silent wharves will never again witness fleets of steamships bound for Bombay and Brisbane, Singapore and Shanghai, Vancouver or Valparaiso.

There was a time, not too long ago, when most of Glasgow's public clocks stopped working. The city seemed to be slumbering, caught in the 19th century and unsure whether to bother waking up for the 20th. When it did awake, it was with the bleary-eyed fervour of someone about to miss breakfast. The city embarked on an orgy of motorway and high-rise building as it dashed to catch up with the times. But it forgot to wash and it didn't check the correct time. The result was not so much a badly planned day but two decades of unnecessary destruction caused by a modernisation programme whose scale and style were already discredited by the time it was begun.

You cannot entirely blame Glasgow for being seduced by the planners' vision of 'the most modern city in Europe' as they said at the time, ignorant of the fact that they had the finest Victorian one. The same civic pride which built the glorious marble interiors of the City Chambers, combined with post-war optimism and a genuine desire to clear the city's slums, convinced those responsible that they were doing the right thing. But they were wrong. Glasgow's extensive, efficient public tramway system (what a boon that would have been today) was scrapped in favour of buses and motorways. Half-baked planning theories produced dereliction and decay. Protesting voices were ignored. The comprehensive re-development schemes of the 1960s and 1970s had a disastrous effect on Glasgow's Victorian architecture, its townscape and the tenement communities affected. Little interest in and even less respect for the wishes of ordinary people was shown and they were decanted from run-down but vibrant communities into the high-rise jerry-built Utopia we see around us today.

This shoddy catalogue of failure is recognised as such today. The bulldozer approach to town planning has finally been discredited. Glasgow is setting an example to other cities, facing the future with a political will and realism: local and regional authorities, government agencies, housing and tenants' associations, private builders, commerce, industry and architects and planners seem united in their desire to rebuild and restore the city in an enlightened and humane way. Tenement restoration, for example, is proving to be an economic and socially desirable alternative to the wrecker's ball. Widespread stone-cleaning has revealed a 19th-century city of honey coloured and red sandstone tenements, ornate civic and ebullient commercial buildings of outstanding quality. Glasgow has washed off its industrial grime. The clocks are working again.

This dramatic *volte-face* has had a tremendous psychological effect on Glasgow's people and on visitors who might only have known the city for its old, unsavoury reputation. By restoring its Victorian heritage and through robust promotion of its good points the city is now perceived in a new and positive light. However, the notion put about that Glasgow will become a garden city, sanitised, post-industrial and populated by happy shoppers is clearly preposterous. It is still an industrial city and too large to rely on services alone for its prosperity. This idea smacks of the misguided idealism which 20 years ago proclaimed comprehensive re-development with equal fervour. Glasgow oughtn't to be deluded by its new, flattering self-image. The reality of declining industry, the lack of a truly Scottish identity by which it might be better known abroad and the problems of its peripheral housing schemes are too serious to be ignored.

Nevertheless, the city has been astonishingly transformed in the last few years. It buzzes with activity and confidence and is beginning to flourish as it has not done since the turn-of-the-century. It is even being vigorously promoted as a tourist and conference centre and not without some justification. Glasgow is the artistic, commercial and industrial capital of Scotland. As the centre of a conurbation of over 2 million people it has a range of museums and art galleries, theatres, cinemas, shops and restaurants to rival any comparable city in Europe. Indeed, its status has been so revived that it has been appointed European City of Culture 1990.

Glasgow, though, is still a city of vivid visual contrasts — New York almost in its mixture of opulence and dilapidation as much as it is in its feisty but friendly population. And there is something reassuring in this. The city is unlikely to be totally bowdlerised by marketing men. Its character and spirit are too deeply ingrained. Children still ask me, 'Are you an artist, mister?' when I'm out drawing. I get offered cups of tea on cold, tenement days. The city's Italian cafés serve the best ice cream in town. Fur-hatted, bourgeois ladies gossip in the Willow Tearooms. Wee wifies frequent the bingo halls on rainy days. School parties spend Impressionistic afternoons at the Art Galleries, pantomimes are sold out at Christmas and bargain hunters invade the Barras at the weekend. City boosters boast of grand (nowadays, cultural) plans. In stubborn Govan men still Clyde-build bulk carriers. Jaywalkers glare at cars and equally stubborn citizens still call the underground the Subway. In the canyons of the city centre Victorian opulence lends a theatrical air to the hum-drum of commerce and banking. Faded grandeur is all around. Business deals are muttered in bars. *Evening Times* reporters expose scams and rackets. Carry-outs still come in three varieties, Chinese, Indian and alcoholic, and you still get rowdiness at football games. Glasgow may have rough edges but it has a warm heart. Built by buccaneering capitalists yet traditionally egalitarian, it is a city with a personality as varied as its architecture.

Robin Ward, January 1988.

Glasgow is a city of tenements. Once scorned as dilapidated symbols of an older order their architectural merits are now being appreciated. These buildings give Glasgow its unique architectural character. They stride up and down the city's hilly topography and line its streets in mesmerisingly long perspectives with a robust dignity characteristic of the Victorian age when they were built.

They don't all look like Charing Cross Mansions. This is the ultimate in Glasgow tenement design — an elaborate 1891 apartment block sweeping majestically into Sauchiehall Street with an architectural panache typical of its time. It was designed by J J Burnet, one of Glasgow's most eminent Victorian architects. Burnet later visited America and subsequently developed a bold Chicago-style modernism which distinguishes many early 20th-century Glasgow commercial buildings, but with Charing Cross Mansions he made a grand Victorian gesture.

The building's rambling façade is anchored at the centre by fine sculptural detail around the large clock face and by an inventive eaves gallery whose tiled recesses ripple round the curved sandstone façade. The whole composition is gift-wrapped with a flourish — a Parisian roofline tipped with cast-ironwork, some very Glasgow chimneys and an elegantly set double-headed cupola. Overall, the building rather resembles the Hôtel de Ville in Paris which Burnet must have seen while studying in that city. In the foreground the terracotta Cameron Fountain, made by the Doulton Company in 1896 in French Renaissance style, adds a further Gallic touch to the Charing Cross area.

Charing Cross Mansions survived the early 1970s turmoil of motorway construction in the area. The M8 Ring Road actually runs in a tunnel between it and the Cameron Fountain (which still leans at an inebriated angle as a result). Both the Fountain and Charing Cross Mansions have been stone-cleaned and restored. Although the Fountain's plumbing still doesn't work, the Mansion's clock now tells the right time.

BANK of SCOTLAND

ANGLO SCOTTISH AIR. SAVERS

ANGLO SCOTTISH TRAVEL | G.E. Williamson Cameras | Royal Bar

City Centre A804

CHARING CROSS BRANCH

ST GEORGES ROAD

Stirling Edinburgh Carlisle M8

SAUCHIEHALL STREET

European Cities

HIGHLAND EXPRESS TORONTO VENICE

ALL YOUR PHOTOS PROCESSED £2.29

OPEN 'TILL 4.45

City Centre A804

Ring Road Greenock Glasgow Airport M8

Meter Zone

St George's X

DAILY RECORD LATE NIGHT SOCCER ACTION

This 1911 building in Cowcaddens is an unusual varia-
tion on the tenement theme. The front end and ground
floor is a branch of the Savings Bank of Glasgow. Above
and at the rear are several Victorian flats. The bank's
presence explains the huge dome and the doorway decorated with sculpture, heraldic devices and granite
columns — banks always had architectural aspira-
tions. When it came to impressing depositors with
architectural good taste, not to mention ornamental
excess for such a normally restrained profession,
money spent on stonework was no object.

The Savings Bank commissioned a notably elaborate group of bank branches in Glasgow around the turn-
of-the-century of which the Cowcaddens building was
the last to be erected. All were built on prominent
corner sites and they all survive today — at Govan,

Shawlands, Bridgeton, Parkhead, Anderston and Cowcaddens — as branches of the TSB. These well-maintained buildings display delightful period details like the weather vane, curved iron balconies, tilework and etched glass windows with original Savings Bank typography at Cowcaddens.

Now a relic of a past era this building still sits confidently on its gushet site — a busy tramway junction before the area was flattened by the urban motorway. Then the Savings Bank seemed to lean forward like a Clydebuilt ship parting a sea of traffic on New City Road. Today it stands in solitary grandeur, a beached liner on a deserted shore.

St George's Cross is another city neighbourhood which was catastrophically touched by the construction of the urban motorway. It is now recovering from years of neglect and planning blight, a recovery symbolised by the restoration of this superb tenement at the corner of Gt Western Road and Maryhill Road. Clarendon Court was built in 1841 by an Edinburgh architect who imported something of the 'Athens of the North' to Glasgow's West End by turning the corner with a giant Greek portico.

A more straightforward Glasgow tenement looms up in the background with a vigorous elegance typical of these commonplace buildings. Glasgow's tenement houses possess an architectural nobility which is absent in the mass-housing of other 19th-century cities. Also of interest here is the cast-ironwork on the public toilet, an unromantic utility perhaps, showing the lengths to which the Victorians went to make the humdrum of daily life, in this case spending a penny, a more edifying experience. These public lavatories with their flowery cast-iron were once as common in Glasgow as the *pissoirs* were in Paris. They are fast disappearing and I have moved this one slightly from its actual position to show it in greater detail.

Glasgow's tenement designers really knew how to turn their corners. They had a feeling for the cityscape, for counterpoint and the arresting detail as they led the eye from street to street. This restored 1853 range in Minerva Street is a fine example. Four storeys high with a well-proportioned façade topped with a pattern of chimney pots, it has the added grandeur of Corinthian pilasters and ground floor arches where the corner swings round into Argyle Street.

This is a spectacular array of turn-of-the-century tenements dominated by an elaborate Edwardian Savings Bank branch. There's an almost Ruritanian flavour to the assembly of turrets, cupolas, balustrades and gables which belies the fact that the East End was once the industrial heart of the city. Architecturally, Parkhead Cross is the best preserved of these neighbourhood meeting points. People, traffic and even the buildings, if you walk around and view the Cross from different angles, seem to ebb and flow across the five point junction. There's a real urban *frisson* here. The rhythm of the city.

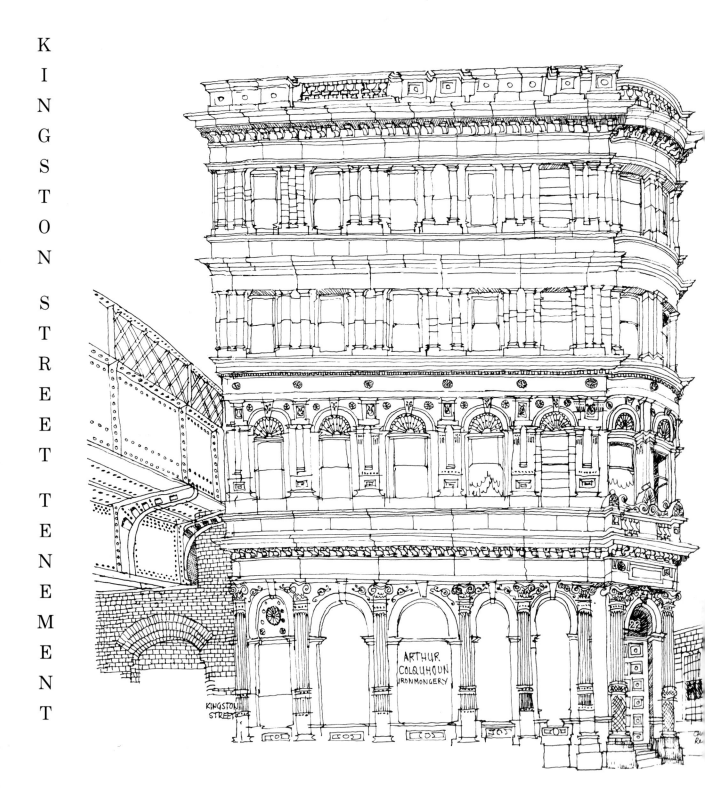

Although the word 'tenement' became synonymous with slums, especially in Glasgow's notorious Gorbals, these buildings are a traditional and respectable Scottish form of urban dwelling. They reached their height of architectural expression in 19th-century Glasgow. Usually four storeys high, 'as high as a coalman could reasonably be expected to climb', their consistent scale and architectural style (based on the proportions of Italian Renaissance *palazzos*) give Glasgow's streets a European rather than English urban quality. Glaswegians visiting Vienna or Milan can feel instantly at home among streets of noble tenements and the collective life which they create. This is the virtue of these buildings. They fostered a real sense of community, where every man's home was not his castle but a shared urban experience. The general friendliness and egalitarian attitude of the average Glaswegian has, to some extent, its roots here. Even suburban dwellers have usually experienced tenement life and it is worth noting that if this spirit of Glasgow is to survive it is tenements, not Noddy houses, which should be built within the city. It is the tenements which established Glasgow's unique social and visual character.

This community spirit was swept away where the 1960s comprehensive re-development schemes were imposed and it is as difficult to forgive the perpetrators' their high-minded ignorance as it is to resurrect the vibrant communities which they destroyed. In the Gorbals even the street plan has been wiped off the map such was the determination to eliminate the symbol, rather than the causes, of poverty. Some buildings survive in this still dilapidated area. The elaborately detailed 1884 tenement, the empty Art Deco warehouse and the exotically named Café del Rio in the drawing are examples. And there are signs of revival here. This tenement and a nearby Art Nouveau example have been restored, the small population of tradesmen and shopkeepers has been joined by an architects' practice and the 1930s Café del Rio by a trendy diner and a wine merchant. But for the moment, heard as the trains rumble over the river, the pulse of the city beats elsewhere.

One of the most encouraging aspects of Glasgow's renaissance has been the return of city centre living. There
has been a sudden re-population of the inner and central areas of Glasgow encouraged by a combination of
enlightened planning, public funding, private initiat-
ive and investment and the desire of many people to
live an urban, rather than a suburban, life. Tenements
have been refurbished, new flats are being built and
empty warehouses, like this splendid 19th-century
example in Montrose Street, converted into bijou
apartments. The alacrity with which these new dwell-
ings have been snapped up is further evidence of the
failure of post-war planning to meet the needs of ordinary people.

Many areas in and around the city centre have been
remarkably transformed. The old Merchant City, a
neglected area of warehouses, small businesses and
tradesmen, has been saved from decay. Pioneers like
the Café Gandolfi have been joined by wine bars, restaurants, late-night delis, picture framers and artists
and designers opening studios and boutiques in the
Victorian and Art Deco warehouses. The former Fruit
Market and many other buildings have been stone-
cleaned and restored. The Scottish National Orchestra
plays in the City Hall. The Glasgow Herald's move to
Albion Street has ensured the preservation of the landmark 1930s Daily Express Building. Even some of the
older businesses usually moved on by such activity
have been encouraged to remain, sustained by the
economic resurgence all around. What has been restored here is not just old buildings but the metropol-
itan bustle, the romantic disorder, the buzz which gives
city life its excitement and unique quality.

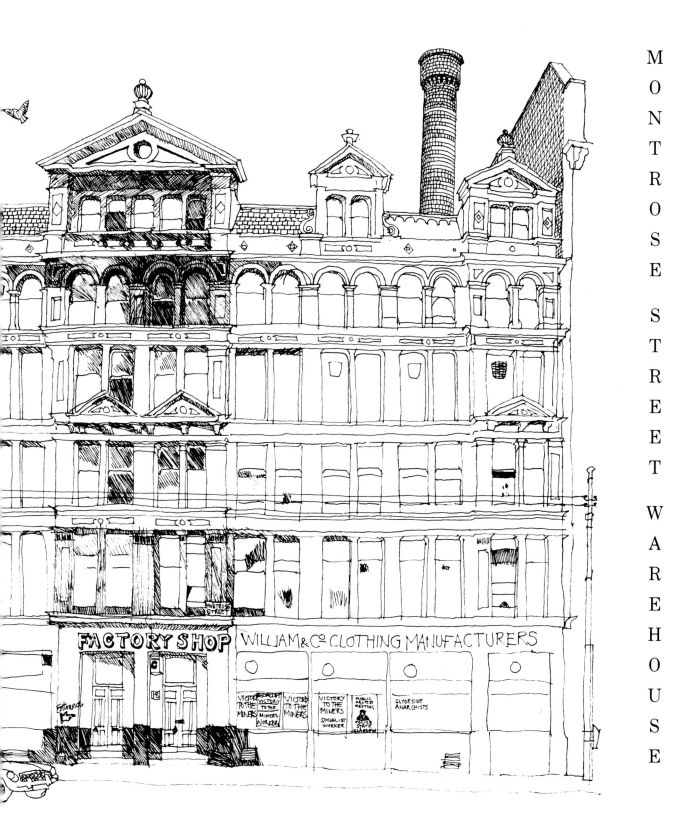

FACTORY SHOP WILLIAM & Co CLOTHING MANUFACTURERS

The 1875 Cooper's Building is a Great Western Road landmark which has recently been restored to its former splendour. Once what the Victorians would have called a 'High Class Provision Merchant' this old grocer's shop now has new flats upstairs and, believe it or not, a 'south of the border', Mexican border that is, cantina. While this might not have amused the Victori-

ans, old buildings lend themselves to this sort of conversion which is preferable to knocking them down (the Art Deco Hubbard's Tearooms across the road is also now a bar). Their ambience is, at least, preserved and often enlivened. Hubbard's is Hollywood in the 1930s. Cooper's now has a colonial swagger.

The Kibble Palace in the Botanic Gardens is one of Glasgow's outstanding Victorian buildings: a 'Crystal Palace of Art' . . . 'a magnificent hall for music or public speaking' . . . decorated with 'celebrated statuary'. It was originally built (c.1863) by engineer and horticulturist John Kibble on his estate on the shores of Loch Long and re-erected in Glasgow in 1873 as a conservatory-cum-concert hall.

A delightful but, I have to say, apocryphal story tells of the 'hidden orchestra'. It apparently played in a watertight chamber, submerged below a large pond in the Palace's central arena. This ingenious arrangement allowed visitors to be serenaded as they walked among the sub-tropical plants by invisible performers! Although the concealed orchestra never played the Kibble Palace retains a magical atmosphere. Its marble statuary can still be seen, artfully posed, among the ferns and cast-iron columns. Glasgow's 19th-century plutocrats would perambulate here sheltered from the weather — a sensation of genteel pleasure which can still be felt in the steamed-up interior beneath the building's graceful, glazed domes.

It is significant that John Kibble was an engineer. Many of the Victorian buildings which are admired today for their modern, indeed, timeless quality and structural virtuosity were the work of engineers, not architects. The great conservatories, the railway stations, bridges and arcades of the 19th century remind us of a time when the engineer was the king of construction.

Glasgow has a fine collection of church towers and steeples which punctuate the city's skyline. In some areas they once jostled for attention with factory chimneys. Today, many have become isolated beacons of faith and humanity amidst the high-rise flats. But in the West End and on the South Side they remain much as built among the tenements and terraces of the city's Victorian bourgeoisie. Kelvinside Botanic Gardens Church, for example, still stands comfortably surrounded by a family of Victoriana — the Kibble Palace, Botanic Gardens, Grosvenor Terrace and the tenements of Hillhead.

Now owned by the Bible Training Institute it was originally built in 1862 during the city's rapid westward expansion. By the standards of its day it is an attractive building with a graceful tower sited for maximum impact when seen as part of the perspective of Great Western Road. It also shows the architectural attention which was given to buildings of this type. Churches played a more influential role in their respective communities, and throughout Victorian society generally, than is the case today and congregations would willingly contribute to see their faith gratified and represented in architecture. Many of these buildings are much grander than either the size or location of the congregations required. Botanic Gardens is only one of several 19th-century churches which were built, for various denominations, in the immediate area and which continue to contribute to the West End's well-preserved Victorian character.

The North Italian Gothic of Botanic Gardens Church complements the Venetian Renaissance of Grosvenor Terrace — one of several spectacular Victorian terraces which give Great Western Road the atmosphere of a *fin-de-siècle*, continental boulevard.

Grosvenor Terrace was built in 1855. Venetian architecture was a popular precedent for Victorian Glasgow. The city's merchant princes no doubt saw themselves as the spiritual heirs to the patricians of that earlier city state. They would certainly have been flattered by such a justification for building in the style. At a time when the Victorians would happily copy any style they fancied, Venetian façades in imperial Glasgow were, at least, appropriate.

Grosvenor Terrace may look much as it did in 1855 but one-third of the building is brand new. The Grosvenor Hotel, at the east end of the terrace, was gutted by fire in 1978 leaving part of the façade damaged beyond repair. However, the importance of this building to the architectural character of the area was recognised and Grosvenor Terrace has since been re-built with glass-reinforced concrete panels cast in the original design. This commendable restoration shows what can be done when concern, imagination and funding are available to preserve historic buildings.

West of Charing Cross is one of Glasgow's finest architectural groupings — the skyline towers of Trinity College (1856-61) and Park Church (1856-57). These dramatic towers, like the *campanile* of an Italian hill town, rise above the early Victorian terraces of Woodlands Hill. They dominate an area whose noble streets, flowing over the hill and terminating in the sweep of Park Terrace, perched on a *butte* overlooking Kelvingrove Park, are among the finest examples of 19th-century town planning in Europe.

Park Church was demolished in 1969 but public concern saved the church tower. Even the planners, at the time besotted with plans to bulldoze Victorian Glasgow, conceded the virtue of the church tower in its urban context. Trinity College was also threatened with the same fate and stood empty and neglected for several years. This indifference to the city's incomparable Victorian heritage seems incredible today and this, in itself, is an indication of the encouraging change in attitude which is now evident. Trinity College, for example, has recently been imaginatively converted for commercial and residential use.

29

To climb Woodlands Hill from the east, passing Trinity College and Park Church, circumnavigating Park Circus and to suddenly encounter the precipitous panorama of Kelvingrove Park from Park Terrace is an unforgettable experience. There is nothing like it this side of Vienna. This is 19th-century town planning on an imperial scale.

Glasgow was the Second City of the Empire then so it's not really surprising that this amazing vista should be hidden away in Scotland. On the left, the 1901 Art Galleries, built for the International Exhibition of that year. On the right, the Victorian Gothic tower of Glasgow University on Gilmorehill, the dominant feature on a campus of great architectural interest and variety.

Kelvingrove Park was designed by Charles Wilson (he also designed the terraces on Woodlands Hill and Trinity College) and was described at the time as 'a delightful retreat ... unrivalled as a place for quiet and meditative enjoyment' which it still is today. The weeping ash trees and the monuments to the Boer War and Lord Roberts of Kandahar certainly give the park a meditative, almost sepulchral air. Here, on a misty winter's day, with the distant, metallic echoes from Govan Shipbuilders carried on the clarity of cold air beyond the elaborate silhouette of the Art Galleries, you can imagine this great city at the height of its imperial power and confidence.

31

The congregation of Cunninghame Free Church in Ballater Street seem to have little to be thankful for. In fact, there is no congregation. They've vanished, as if struck by the plague. The traditional tenement community which existed in this area has been scattered by

comprehensive re-development and this attractive church, its fanciful cupola like a flower in a wasteland, has since been demolished.

Rated alongside, say, Trinity College, its architectural qualities are debatable but like many minor buildings it gained stature in the context of its surroundings. This consideration is too often overlooked. Even if an older building does not rate a mention in Glasgow's architectural canon this should not guarantee its destruction.

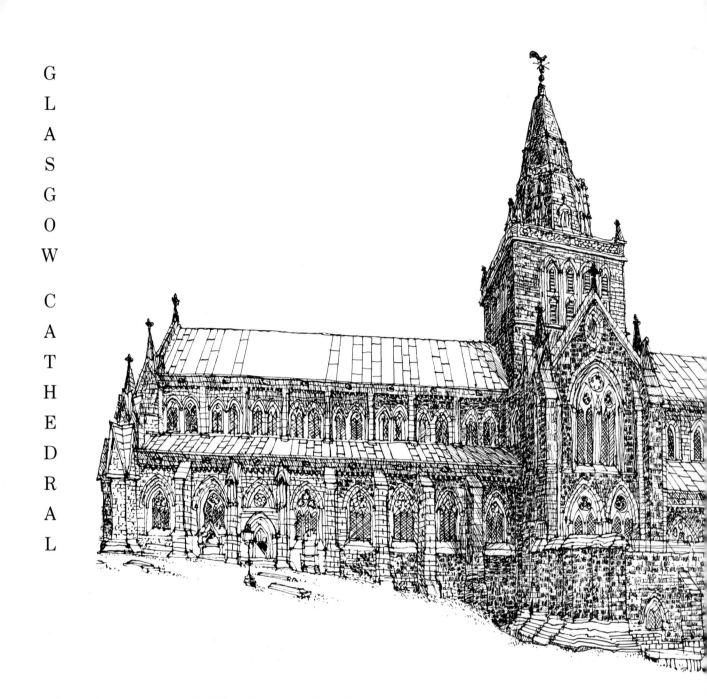

The most venerable building in Glasgow is the Cathedral most of which dates from the 13th century. Built on high ground to the east of the present-day city centre on land dedicated to St Mungo, Glasgow's patron saint, it once dominated medieval Glasgow much as St Paul's, on a grander scale, rose above 17th-century London. Today it is lost amidst a clutter of 19th and 20th-century development and is best seen from the south or east where rising ground heightens its presence. It then begins to command the area around it as a great cathedral should.

Glasgow Cathedral is one of the oldest and finest medieval churches in Scotland. Many were destroyed during the Reformation but Glasgow's cathedral survived the depredations of that time. It has also survived architectural alterations and additions over the years and retains a visual balance and sober, if solemn,

dignity. Its Gothic style is plain, unadorned, stoic and Scottish rather than flowery and Continental. The heavily buttressed exterior not only braces the building but also seems to defy the harsh northern climate. Inside the Cathedral's silent, vaulted interior there is a pervasive, unsettling sense of antiquity. There is no pious self-righteousness here, only the noble melan-

choly of old stones conveying the hope and faith of the Cathedral's builders tempered by the wisdom and dismay of time. This startling quality is reinforced by the colours of Scottish regiments which hang in the nave, the wall plaques commemorating imperial soldiers and the stained-glass windows representing biblical scenes, battles and now vanished local trades and industries.

There is no lack of self-righteousness above the Cathedral where Glasgow's 18th and 19th-century merchants and industrialists commemorated themselves on an astonishing hill-top necropolis. Here, row upon row, as they tumble down the hillside, the sententious tombstones of the city's commercial aristocracy display every 19th-century architectural style found in the city which they overlook. Unlike the Cathedral, there is no reflective edification prompted here — only the thought of wealthy Victorians' ability to meet their maker with more money, vulgarly spent, than good taste or humility.

This is St Vincent Street Church (1857-59) designed by Glasgow's most original and talented architect of the mid-Victorian era, Alexander 'Greek' Thomson. 'Greek' Thomson never travelled far himself but he was undoubtedly influenced by Victorian travellers' tales of Empire and by the contemporary interest in the antiquities of Greece and Egypt.

The Victorians, unsure of their cultural identity in a time of industrial change, looked to the past for aesthetic advice. They freely used any obsolete architectural style they thought would confer a surface of good taste and dignity on their buildings and on themselves. This practice resulted in the amazing profusion of styles which a Victorian city like Glasgow exhibits. Few architects did anything other than imitate the glory of Greece, Rome or Egypt. But Thomson interpreted a worn-out style in an original way as St Vincent Street Church demonstrates.

The building occupies a steeply sloping site which allowed Thomson to erect a breathtaking series of plinths, porticos and pediments which culminate in an exotic Indian/Egyptianesque tower. It looks as if it was designed for some Mogul potentate rather than for the United Presbyterian Church. There seems little stern, presbyterianism represented here. Yet the attitude which guided Thomson throughout his career was stern and rigorous. He refused to work in any other style and there is a logic, an almost Calvinistic rigour, underpinning his academic but adventurous work. This remarkable building is one of the architectural treasures of 19th-century Europe. The modern block behind, although of some distinction, is eclipsed by comparison.

Thomson's Caledonia Road Church (1856-57) ranks just as highly even in its ruined condition following a fire in 1965. Only the portico and tower now remain. In any other city in Europe this building would have been restored but, so far, not in Glasgow. There was a proposal to move it stone-by-stone to the top of Buchanan Street but my own feeling is that it should be left as a ruin, in picturesque decay, like the Acropolis from which Thomson sought inspiration. If the building is ever restored it should be as the centre-piece of a re-planned Gorbals, the sad, empty area where it stands.

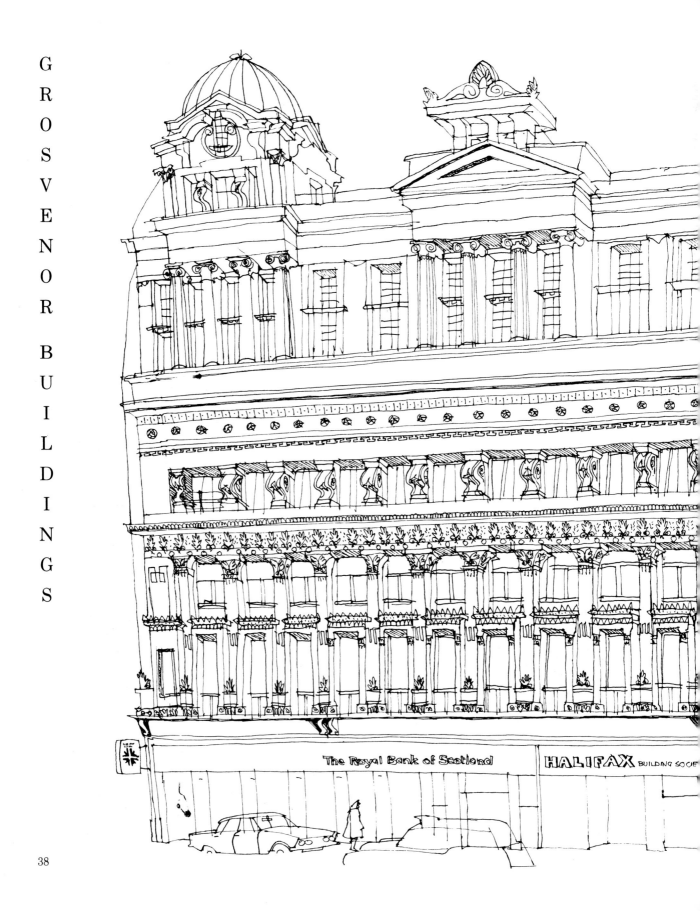

The Royal Bank of Scotland   HALIFAX BUILDING SOCIE

Thomson was a master of structure and proportion. He shunned the undisciplined, decorative excess seen in other Victorian buildings. A closer look, however, reveals that his work is often delicately engraved or carved with Greek or Egyptian motifs. Grosvenor Buildings (1859-61) in Gordon Street is hand-carved in this way although, from a distance, the façade appears restrained and functional. This meticulous detail speaks straight from the drawing board. You feel that Thomson was up there on a ladder doing it himself. The ungainly Baroque top part of the building is not Thomson's work. It was added in 1907 long after his death. Yet this mock-palatial pile of stone, far from spoiling the dignity of the Thomson structure below, only makes itself look pompous by comparison.

'Greek' Thomson could have been called 'Egyptian' — his buildings have as many Egyptian features as Greek. One warehouse is even called Egyptian Halls. It's in Union Street and was built in 1871-73. His Greco/Egyptianesque motifs again appear inscribed on the façade, while the eaves gallery (a Thomson trademark) has a troupe of chubby Egyptian columns propping up the heavy cornice overhang. Thomson's eye for proportion is clearly shown in this building — the conflicting vertical and horizontal elements of the composition have been resolved in a masterly way.

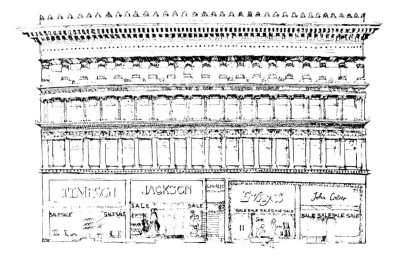

Warehouses may not seem architecturally promising but the Victorians treated them as they did other buildings, lavishly decorating them in fashionable styles. The Ca d'Oro Building (1872 re-built 1988) originally a furniture warehouse in Union Street is a spectacular example of this. The façade, saved after a fire in 1987, is made almost entirely of cast-iron.

The structural use of iron and steel in Victorian times was a great technological leap forward, leading the way for the steel-framed tall buildings we are familiar with today. Although normally associated with epic structures like the Eiffel Tower or the Forth Railway Bridge, where the iron and steelwork were boldly exposed, both materials were used in Victorian buildings but hidden behind masonry façades. Only a few architects realised the full potential of iron and steel. Cast-iron, for example, could be moulded to mass-produce arches, cornices, doorways, columns — even entire façades — in complex decorative patterns. The Venetian-style Ca d'Oro shows the wonderful lightness and grace which repeating patterns of cast-iron and glass could achieve.

Cast-iron buildings were popular in America during this time. New York foundries mass-produced Venetian-style 'iron-fronts'. Many still exist there. Others were shipped west on the railroads to be assembled piece-by-piece in cowboy towns on the prairies. In Europe, Glasgow pioneered this type of building and several fine examples still survive including the best of all — the 'Iron Building' (page 4) in Jamaica Street.

Built in 1855-56, Gardner's Iron Building was designed by John Baird. Here, the Venetian arches are beautifully proportioned, pointing to the elegant steelwork of the best functional buildings of the 20th-century. Structurally advanced for its time Gardner's is of great historical importance. If Glasgow had a list of 'top ten buildings' this one would be on it. Its delicate iron and glass façade (which even has retained its original lettering) is maintained in immaculate condition by Martin & Frost, its new owners.

During the 19th century Glasgow's foundries produced tons of cast-ironwork. Walter MacFarlane's evocatively named Saracen Foundry at Possilpark even published a mail order catalogue full of cast-iron fountains, columns, balustrades, lamp-posts, doorways and arcades. Complete buildings could be assembled from the MacFarlane catalogue. If you wanted a People's Palace style Winter Garden in, say, Melbourne, they would ship it out to you. In fact, you can still find more Glasgow cast-iron work in former colonies like India or Australia than in the city itself.

Much of Glasgow's decorative cast-iron was melted down during the war to make battleships (or so the propaganda said). Fortunately, some pieces still exist like the fountain opposite the People's Palace on Glasgow Green (page 3). This was cast by MacFarlane's and is a typically florid example of the work which this company produced. It's an exotic little structure, slightly Moorish, suggesting the alcàzars of southern Spain.

The People's Palace is exactly that — built in 1898 to 'make cultural provision for the city's working classes'. It was hugely popular when first opened, its cast-iron and glass Winter Garden a Kibble Palace of the East End. The ethos behind the founding of the People's Palace may sound patronising today but it was a characteristic and successful example of enlightened Victorian philanthropy. Re-development of the surrounding area caused attendances to fall but people are

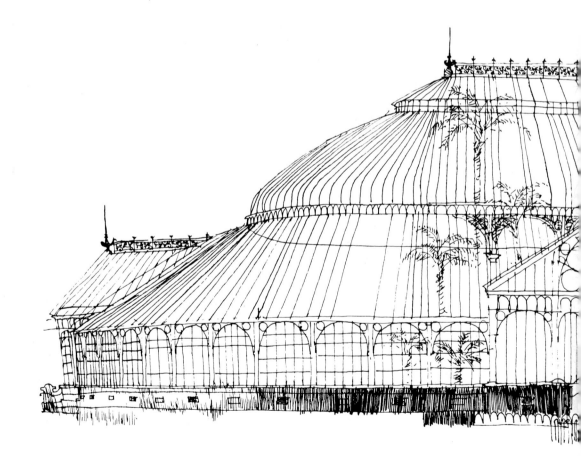

moving back and the building is again assuming its social significance and historical importance.

The People's Palace Museum has a large collection of Glaswegiana helped, ironically, by the haste and scale of demolition during the 1960s and 1970s and by the presence nearby of the 'Barras', Glasgow's boisterous weekend market, a rich source of bric-a-brac. The museum also tells, with force and vigour, the story of workers' struggles and of the Bolshevism which swept the Clyde shipyards in 1919. At a time when there is an evident tendency to commercialise and package Glasgow's history as a tourist attraction the importance of the People's Palace and the fundamental, essentially Glaswegian, egalitarianism behind its foundation and purpose cannot be over-emphasised.

Many of Glasgow's Victorian magnates had philan-
thropic ideals. They founded libraries, parks and
erected public buildings in their names. The Mitchell
Library, for example, now one of the most extensive
reference libraries in Europe, was founded by Stephen
Mitchell, a Glasgow tobacco merchant, with the stipu-
lation that no one should be barred from using it as a
source of knowledge and information. This egalitarian
attitude is deeply rooted in Glasgow life and, to an
extent, can be credited to the city's enlightened capitalists (those who were) as much as it can to the labour
force. The Pearce Institute at Govan Cross is another
example of plutocratic patronage. It was financed by
Sir William Pearce, a chairman of Fairfield's shipyard,

for the benefit of the people of Govan. Pearce himself, or rather his statue, stands outside, where he beholds his work, an attractive Scottish Renaissance style turn-of-the-century building (1903-05) topped with a model sailing ship. Fairfield's shipyard still exists maintaining a Clyde shipbuilding tradition going back 150 years. Many great ships were built here including the Empress liners for Canadian Pacific, battleships for the Royal Navy and even a yacht for the Tsar of Russia. Now Govan Shipbuilders, the yard has had to specialise and modernise to survive. A phantom image of Victorian industrial grandeur, it maintains, against all the odds, a 'Clydebuilt' presence in advanced marine technology.

The Clyde Trust Building, which overlooks the river at the Broomielaw, is a majestic symbol of Glasgow's maritime past. It still houses the Clyde Port Authority and although little remains of the port the building retains a muscular, Victorian quality. It is lavishly decorated with sculptural groups of Neptune and other seafaring symbols. There are even two ships prows launching themselves from the façade. Inside, there is a splendid period interior.

The Clyde Trust Building was constructed in two stages, the Robertson Street façade in 1883-86 and the domed corner in 1905-08, to Beaux-Arts designs by J J Burnet. It was never completed — Glasgow's decline may have overtaken the port authority's architectural ambitions. It does look lop-sided. Both the pedimented entrance and the domed corner extension seem to have been planned, at different times, as the centrepieces of the composition. However, extensions to the left or right which would have resolved the asymmetry remain un-built, leaving the Clyde Trust Building looking like one of these turn-of-the-century ship models, mounted in a mirrored glass case, which seem complete but which are only half-built reflections. Perhaps some day a mirrored glass neighbour will complete the illusion. Meanwhile, the Clyde Trust Building, recently superbly restored and floodlit, sails on like a ship in the night.

S C W S   B U I L D I N G

At first glance this building looks like a palace or an expensive municipal edifice. It is neither. It's a warehouse. Not an ordinary warehouse but a Victorian one. Only the Victorians could build commonplace structures like warehouses in such a grand and ostentatious manner.

This one (the old Scottish Co-operative Wholesale Society headquarters) in Morrison Street was built in 1879 and designed in rich French Renaissance style by the architects Bruce and Hay. It was rumoured that they had re-used their unsuccessful City Chambers competition submission — a rumour hotly denied by the two architects. Nevertheless, the SCWS building would not look out of place in George Square. It has the further distinction of being so large that it even manages to dwarf the city's urban motorway.

Several fine warehouses in the SCWS group were demolished in the 1970s but Morrison Street, after years of decline, is showing signs of a revival. New tenement houses have been built opposite the SCWS building which, with its surviving neighbours, provide a real sense of place for this new community.

We ought to be grateful to the Victorians for their enlightened folly in designing such marvellously useless decorative façades. These extraordinary buildings contribute considerably to the rich and varied atmosphere of former great industrial cities like Glasgow.

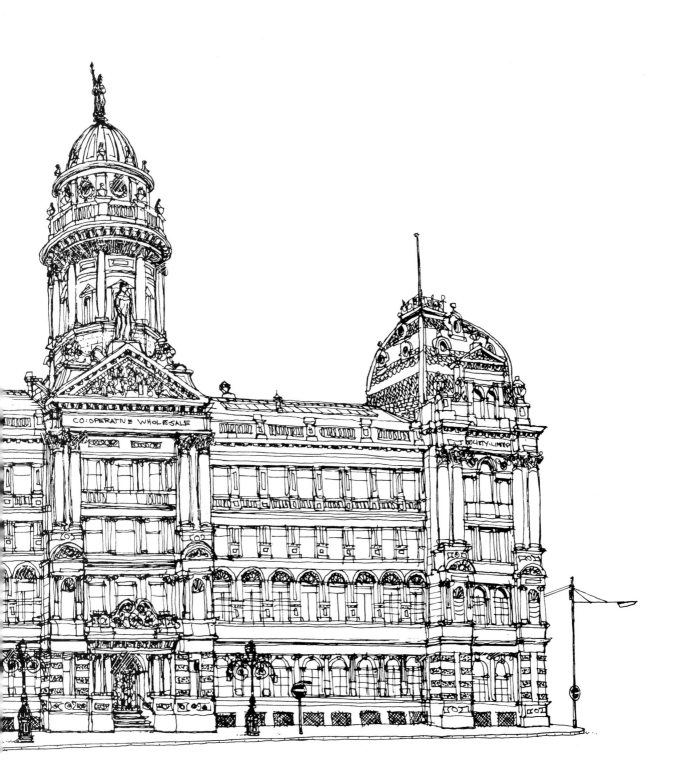

49

Victorian architectural pastiche reached a peak of absurdity in 1889 on Glasgow Green. This is Templeton's Carpet Factory. You expect carpets to be richly decorated and colourful. Here the architect, William Leiper, treated the building in the same way.

Templeton's, as 'patrons of the arts, resolved . . . to erect, instead of the ordinary and common factory, something of permanent architectural interest and beauty.' It has been said that Leiper was asked what he thought was the most admirable building in the world. 'The Doge's Palace in Venice,' he replied. So Templeton's, in the best tradition of autocratic patrons, commanded him to design them a Doge's Palace — on Glasgow Green.

Now whether this multi-coloured brick, tile and mosaic carpet factory is beautiful or not, it is far from being common or ordinary. It is a preposterous architectural joke, an engaging folly. Unlike more pompous Victorian buildings which pretend to be grand opera, Templeton's is genuine — genuine pantomime that is. It's a wonderful building, quite out of character in a city of grand Victorian stone façades and has recently been restored and converted to become the Templeton Business Centre, part of the city's ambitious East End renewal.

Another fancy-dress façade in Glasgow can be seen on the former Fish Market on Clyde Street. It is also an example of adventurous re-use of a redundant old building. Behind the French baroque exterior a spacious, 19th-century cast-iron market hall has been sensitively adapted as a shopping/restaurant complex. The interior of the 'Briggait', as it's now called, has kept something of its Victorian market flavour while the façade retains its period details — banded columns, winged sea-horses, and plaques of Queen Victoria.

Peeping above the roof of this exuberant 1873 waterfront building is the mid-17th-century Merchants' Steeple, topped with a model sailing ship weathervane. City merchants once used the steeple as a crow's-nest to spot their ships approaching Glasgow's upper harbour. A further reminder of Glasgow's maritime past is the 'Carrick', a 19th-century sailing ship, formerly a wool clipper on the Australian trade, which is permanently berthed nearby.

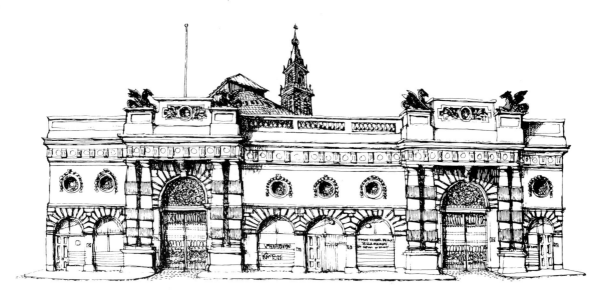

Within the illustration:

BAXTER BROS GLASGOW LTD

TOY STATIONERY

Greenock
Glasgow
Airport

Edinburgh
Stirling
Carlisle

M8   M8

Diversion

GOODS ENTR.

BABY
WEAR

COOK STREET   BRADESTON

52

Glasgow's minor industrial buildings, utilitarian, usually solidly built in stone or red-brick patterned in Italianate style, tend to be overlooked. Conservation seems to pass them by. Yet they are almost always attractive and ideal for conversion to other uses — artists' studios, flats or small offices and workshops. Templeton's Carpet Factory has already been converted for small firms and other buildings of this type could be similarly re-used.

While none can match the architectural burlesque of Templeton's, this 1900 warehouse in Tradeston Street does make the stage. Dressed in Italian Gothic, the brickwork detail is particularly well-handled especially at cornice level and on the Florentine tower, the eye-catching feature which distinguishes this underrated building. I hope it doesn't follow Kingston Grain Mills (page 96) built in 1875 nearby. This had a wonderful Moorish/Byzantine pattern of red and white brickwork looking like something out of the Arabian Nights. A jewel in the desert of demolition all around, it could have been polished and restored. It was torn down in 1978.

The banks of the Forth and Clyde canal were once dominated by Glasgow's most impressive example of industrial architecture. This was Pinkston Power Station at Port Dundas. This monumental, twin-chimneyed, red-brick building was constructed in 1900 for the electrification of the city's tramway system. It is a building of operatic, even Hollywood proportions. You can imagine a cast of thousands, thousands of brickies that is, putting it together. Its skyscraping chimneys could be seen from miles away and the building unequivocably conveyed an overpowering expression of its purpose, characteristic of the best industrial architecture of its day.

Pinkston, sadly, is now only a memory, like the extensive and efficient tramway system which it powered. No further use could be found for it when it closed and it was demolished in the late 1970s. That Glasgow is no longer primarily an industrial city should not excuse the destruction of monuments of that time, especially when they are of Pinkston's peerless quality. The surviving Barclay Curle engineering hall at Scotstoun is an example worth considering in this respect.

THE FINNIESTON CRANE

Some day, if it survives long enough, the Finnieston Crane will become a tourist attraction like the Pyramids of Egypt or the Colosseum in Rome. Future Glaswegians and visitors will gaze on it with awe and wonder. Certainly, this giant piece of engineering is an appropriate reminder of Glasgow's vanished industrial empire. It was designed to load steam locomotives, which came down from Springburn on low-loaders, for export overseas and is still occasionally used for boilers and other heavy loads.

To the left of the crane is the North Rotunda entrance and lift shaft of the 1905 Clyde Harbour Tunnel. A twin structure stands on the south bank. The tunnel, with its white-tiled interior and wood-panelled elevators down which pedestrians and vehicles plumbed mysterious, Piranesian depths beneath the river, was an evocative Victorian relic. It was recently closed and, like the docks, filled in, controversial and short-sighted decisions in view of current and anticipated recreational and residential activity on both banks of the river, which may prove to be regrettable. Having said that, the North Rotunda has been saved from demolition and been converted into a waterfront bar and restaurant, as has the former Queen's Dock pumping station, a handsome Italianate building nearby.

St Enoch Station was built in the 1870s for the Glasgow and South Western Railway. Raised above street level, it lent a real air of excitement and anticipation to the routine of arriving and departing by train. It was a romantic railway palace flamboyantly reflecting the spirit of its age. The huge Gothic St Enoch Hotel concealed a magnificent, arched train shed, an engineering spectacle of elegant grandeur — one of the finest in Europe.

However, no further use could be found for either the hotel or the station train shed — except to pull them down and deposit the rubble of the hotel in Queens Dock to prepare that site for the new Scottish Exhibition and Conference Centre. The train shed's iron went to the scrapyard. St Enoch Station was suggested as a suitable building to be converted to become the new exhibition centre but this imaginative idea was ignored. That this proposal could have been achieved is shown in Manchester where the former Central Station has been converted for exhibition use and the adjacent hotel refurbished, all with great success. Only the whimsical Jacobean style St Enoch Subway Station, built in 1896, remains in this view today.

The SEC could be forgiven being built on the grave of St Enoch if it was a better building. Regrettably it squanders the potential of its waterfront site. It should have had the presence of a great ship — multilayered with decks and setbacks and cavernous halls — signalling its arrival in Glasgow with clever reference to the city's history. While it has undoubtedly raised the city's commercial profile, architecturally Glasgow and Scotland deserve better.

The new St Enoch shopping centre manages some architectural and engineering quality, particularly in the bravura steelwork, but here too shows a lack of vision. The building resembles a pyramid from some angles but fails to make a bold, memorable statement. It should have been a real pyramid, steel and glass, ten or twenty storeys high, housing, not the relics of the Pharoahs but the loot of the material world, a land-

mark building with ironic reference to the spirit of our times. It would certainly have given architectural stature to Glasgow's much touted re-emergence as a great city. Without new buildings of real quality that re-emergence will remain just that — much touted. There is no substitute for imagination and an emphasis on quality when commissioning modern buildings.

ST ENOCH SQUARE

The 19th-century railway companies had architecturally exalted views of their own importance. They saw themselves as ambassadors of a new age, as dynamic and powerful as the fire-eating locomotives which hauled their trains. They matched this view in the cathedral-like stations which they built all over Europe and America. Despite the new iron and steel technology with which the stations were built, the Victorian railway barons commissioned monumental station façades to look like Greek temples, Florentine *palazzos,* French *châteaux* and Gothic cathedrals — any historical style which would confer nobility and prestige on their works.

Glasgow's Central Station and Central Hotel are typical. Built for the Caledonian Railway in 1884, the hotel was designed in what can best be described as Scots/Scandinavian Renaissance style — an amazing clutter of gables and windows, surmounted by a tall clocktower from which you can tell the time from miles away. Particularly attractive is the glazed cast-iron canopy in the forecourt which still displays its original Caledonian lettering. However, the true architecture of the railway age survives in the impressive iron and glass canopies which leap in graceful arches or girders across smoky, sun-dappled platforms. A marvellous, sprawling canopy can be found inside Central Station.

The Central Hotel has been stone-cleaned and the station interior refurbished. The refurbishment has been sensitively achieved and includes new shops which echo the Edwardian style of the station's wooden offices and news-stands and help preserve its period character. A sad loss, though, was the huge wooden train indicator board. It looked like the bridge of a ship and was operated by a crew of railwaymen who manually displayed large destination signs. It was replaced recently by a gigantic, ugly electronic board. Had the old, efficient and legible system been retained (the ship's bridge still exists) Glasgow Central would have become a place of pilgrimage for rail buffs everywhere.

THE CITY CHAMBERS

Glasgow's City Chambers is a Victorian town hall to eclipse all others. Like the Victorian railway stations buildings of this type were intended to impress. They were manifestations of municipal pride and prestige. Glasgow, if the City Chambers is anything to go by, must have had something to be proud about and it did. Glasgow was the Second City of the British Empire and in the 1880s it needed a new administration building to enhance this reputation.

The building was the result of two competitions. The eventual winner, which stands in George Square, was designed in Baroque/Renaissance style by William Young, a London Scot. It was begun in 1883 and inaugurated by Queen Victoria herself in 1888. An elaborate extension in similar style was added behind in 1923-26.

The composition of the façade and the relationship of the tower and corner domes to the rest of the building are well handled. The façade is covered with ornamental detail — bas-relief tableaux and sculptural groupings — but skilfully avoids over-ostentation. Until you venture inside, that is.

Beyond the gilded iron gateways there is a Victorian interior of staggering opulence. There are grand stairways of Carrara marble rising three floors, Venetian glass and mosaics, Spanish mahogany fittings, Scottish granite, stained glass, brilliantly coloured tiled corridors, a sumptuous banqueting hall and a lobby looking like a church of the Italian Renaissance. Altogether it is a building of baroque splendour. The architect hoped that the City Chambers would be '. . . one of the most lasting monuments which they (Glasgow's citizens) will leave to tell to future generations of the marvellously rapid growth and energy of the city . . .' He wasn't far wrong.

To understand just how fortunate Glasgow is in the architectural quality of the City Chambers you only have to look at the Art Galleries. Built for the 1901 International Exhibition it is the sort of hotch-potch which the late Victorians tended to design. This was a time when their self-confidence was not always matched by good taste. Its façade is clumsily clustered with mock-Renaissance details and pompous her-

aldry, topped by a zany *mélange* of towers and cupolas. From some angles it reminds me of buildings on Vienna's Ringstrasse while the two main towers have a Spanish-colonial quality. Architecturally pure it is not.

Architectural purists have a lot to sniff about here. And they have done a lot of sniffing over the years — the building has been consistently under-rated. It has aged

gracefully and it has its merits. Even the leaden interior (which houses Britain's best civic art collection and includes a superb group of French Impressionists) has a basically sound plan which manipulates space and perspective to some effect. It has been said that the Art Galleries were built the wrong way round, the main entrance facing south instead of north. This may seem true today but the original main entrance (shown in this drawing) did face north, planned to face into the 1901 exhibition area. No criticism of the building, however, can deny its most memorable feature — the eccentric arrangement of towers and cupolas which, particularly when seen on a misty day or at sunset, are romantic and capture the confidence and conceit of the late Victorian era.

If the Art Galleries goes over the top it has nothing on this Disneyesque fantasy — the Christian Institute in Bothwell Street. It was built in several stages between 1877 and 1898. The original centre section was designed in Romanesque style later flanked by two massive Gothic wings housing a YMCA hotel on the left and the Bible Training Institute on the right. American evangelists were said to have played a part in its early life and the building certainly makes up in architectural zeal what it lacks in refinement. Inside, the floor and window levels were in constant conflict and the façade presented a mis-match of towers and gables. And yet the building carried its ineptitude with a certain panache. It was a glorious Gothic folly. To many, its exuberance possessed no architectural merit and it was demolished in 1980 although the façade could and should have been saved. Quite a number of Victorian buildings in Glasgow, the Stock Exchange in Buchanan Street for example, have been preserved with modern interiors built behind the existing façades, thus maintaining the city centre's 19th-century character, without prejudicing the need for modern facilities inside.

Many Glasgow banks and insurance companies built distinguished city centre buildings during the 19th century. They sought to represent their professional dignity and cultural credentials in architecture, a tradition some maintain today (Glasgow's better modern buildings tend to be banks and insurance offices). Architecturally, these Victorian commercial blocks were solid and dependable, with a touch of grandeur designed to convey an impression of confidence and stability. Above all, they were respectable. Occasionally, though, a flamboyant rogue would appear.

Halfway down Hope Street is Glasgow's most raffish insurance building. It has a bewildering complexity of columns, gables, arches, pinnacles and statuary designed to praise and glorify the Liverpool, London and Globe Insurance Company. Who? Well, whoever they were, in 1898 their architectural ambitions were certainly global. Just about every style is here. Remarkably, all the parts of this Victorian architectural jumble sale fit together in a visually satisfying way due to the octagonal, projecting corner tower — a design device employed on many 19th-century Glasgow buildings. Who said insurance was boring?

This building gains further stature by the way it seems to climb up Hope Street, an exciting topographic effect repeated at every other corner where Glasgow's city centre grid plan slides up and down the city's steep, San Francisco-like contours.

While the Liverpool, London and Globe building occupies a large corner block, many late Victorian buildings in Glasgow squeeze onto narrow sites of former Georgian buildings. The North British Rubber Company building (what grand names these Victorian businesses had, evoking, in this case, the plantations of Malaya) stands on a narrow plot in Buchanan Street. Most people walk past the tall façade unaware of the balconies and crow-stepped gables. But when you look up and up, this architectural aria, built in 1898, strikes a resonant, high note which echoes down the lane in reprise.

Glasgow Cross was the original centre of the city before the westward expansion of the 19th century. This is where the tobacco lords would swagger down the Trongate and meet in steamed-up coffee houses to discuss cargo rates from Virginia and receive news of Yorktown. In 1745, Bonnie Prince Charlie paraded his troops here and briefly stayed in a house on the Trongate where the Scottish Baronial style Royal Bank building now stands. It was a rumbustious area of auction houses and markets, churches, grand villas, bordellos and slums.

Something of the vitality of this earlier Glasgow survives here. There is a distinctly Scottish urban feel to the area, enhanced by the Tolbooth Steeple (1626), the

Tron Steeple (c.1600), the crow-step gables of the 19th-century Saltmarket tenements, and the Scottish Baronial style of Anderson's '. . . general and household drapery . . . at the keenest cut prices in all Glasgow . . .' Tron Warehouse. There is still a blustery, friendly vulgarity here of discount shops and the garment trade, tattoo artists and toy shops, taverns and the Tron Theatre. On the periphery of the restored Merchant City, Glasgow Cross has been cleaned up lately. Fortunately, it has not been falsified in expectation of a tourist trade and, like the nearby 'Barras', retains its essentially Glaswegian character — populated by a mix of respectable punters, businessmen, eccentric shopkeepers, wee wifies, assorted drunks and chancers.

Buchanan Street is Glasgow's premier shopping street, Architecturally too, it is of the first order, containing one of the best groups of mixed 19th-century buildings in Britain. From beyond the distant pinnacles of St George's Tron Church (1807) and all the way down to this huge, domed corner which brings Buchanan Street to an emphatic halt at Argyle Street, it is lined with Victorian façades of astonishing variety and quality.

This corner building seen from St Enoch Subway Station was designed by one Horatio Bromhead and built in 1901-03. Its Argyle Street entrance is flanked by two muscular statues which seem to be holding the

building on their shoulders. Enter here and you walk straight into the early 20th-century — along a wood-panelled, barrel-vaulted corridor, through double, brass-handled doors to a tiled stairway and one of these wonderful, old caged elevators with concertina, trellis gates and a patient operator who sits inside. He looks as old as the building. There's a romantic, faded grandeur here (for those who wish see it and which would be lost by over-enthusiastic restoration), an atmosphere which evokes private eyes, shady deals and front companies, silent amidst the bustle of the city.

One of the most attractive buildings in Buchanan Street is this delightful, Dutch-gabled dolls' house built in 1896. Now a branch of the Clydesdale Bank, it was originally a well-known Miss Cranston tearoom and once contained murals by Charles Rennie Mackintosh. Its façade, beautifully detailed in French Renaissance style, is much more delicately handled than on other late-Victorian buildings.

In complete contrast, of the sort which enlivens the architecture of Buchanan Street, the Royal Bank of Scotland building (1850-51) was designed in a classical manner by Charles Wilson. It is refreshingly restrained yet avoids the glum sobriety often found in buildings of this style and type. The scrollwork which twirls along the façade below the cornice line adds a lighthearted touch.

Large department stores were a 19th-century innovation. The first was Bon Marché, built in Paris in 1876. Such was its success in selling an assortment of goods under one roof that the idea was quickly copied across Europe and America.

Architecturally, these stores sought to persuade their customers, through fashionable decoration and contrived atmosphere, of their prestige, good taste and quality. This principle holds true today. Most, whether in London, Paris or Chicago, were sumptuously embellished in palatial styles. Glasgow once boasted several large department stores but, due to changing retail fashions, only a few remain. The saddest loss was the demise of Copland's in Sauchiehall Street, replaced by an unattractive mall in the 1970s.

Many have been altered. Lewis's in Argyle Street retains its 1930s façade but, apart from an Art Deco stairway, little survives of its original interior. Frasers in Buchanan Street, however, is an other story. Here the 1885 galleried main hall survives in its original splendour. It is decorated in Italianate style, its wedding cake plasterwork rising through five floors to a barrel-vaulted, glazed roof, a prototype of the atrium shopping malls of today. This well-maintained 'commercial crystal palace' is one of the finest of its era. Across the street the Argyle Arcade (1827) is also of architectural interest. It too, is well-preserved.

A modern version of Frasers' galleria is Princes Square, opened in Buchanan Street in 1987. This exciting shopping structure roofs over a formerly picturesque but shabby open square between Buchanan Street and Queen Street. The classical east façade of the square is now indoors, the central feature of, believe it or not, an Art Nouveau shopping mall. This is so well designed in its use of space and in the standard of craftsmanship which it exhibits (the Art Nouveau ironwork, the tiled seafood bar, the stained glass and the woodwork) that I find it difficult to sustain my reservations — namely, that we live in the late-20th century and not the Vienna or Brussels of 1900 from

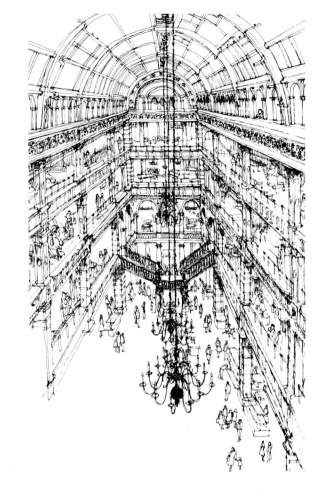

which the décor of Princes Square has been borrowed. It really is a sign of the collapse of confidence in the architecture of our own time that the rare, elegant clarity which can be achieved when a first-rate modern design uses traditional materials (the Burrell building for example) was not attempted here.

Personal opinion aside, this is a fine building. The Art Nouveau may wear well and be an attraction in itself. It certainly is an appropriate style to choose for Glasgow since the city, under the spell of Mackintosh, was one of the major European centres of that style at the turn-of-the-century. Thankfully, the designers of Princes Square have resisted the Mackintosh cliché and used, instead the imagery of the Vienna Secession and Horta's Brussels, thus making a discreet and knowledgeable reference to Mackintosh himself.

77

T H E   H O R S E S H O E   B A R

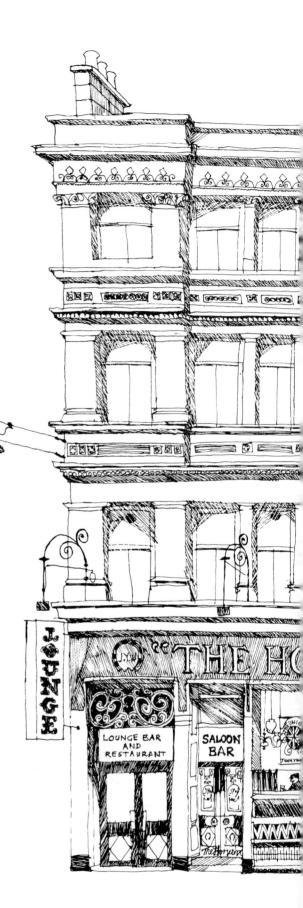

In Glasgow, as elsewhere at the time, the Victorians' delight in decoration was displayed everywhere in their urban environment — from the extravagance of the City Chambers to the everyday tramcars which used to glide along the city's streets. Some of these sedate, palaces-on-wheels can still be seen in Glasgow's excellent Museum of Transport in the Kelvin Hall where you can admire their painted glass, polished woodwork and brass fittings. Even bars were lavishly decorated in palatial style, partly to impress customers who could never achieve such opulence at home and to seem reassuringly familiar to those who did. Bar landlords also hoped that their expensive interior décor might deflect the temperance societies' criticism of seedy drinking joints and rowdy behaviour and encourage a civilised clientele.

These late 19th century 'oases of refreshment' boasted sumptuous interiors: huge carved mahogany

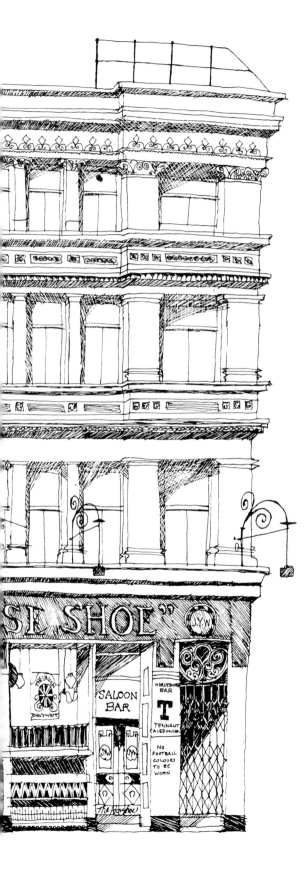

or walnut bars, gilded and engraved mirrors, brass light fittings, decorative tilework, marble tables, granite bar tops, stained or painted glass and imitation plasterwork ceilings held up by ornate cast-iron columns. Changing fashions have seen many of these Victorian bars altered and, more recently, imitated. Fortunately, a few splendid, original examples have survived. One of the best, dating from the 1880s, is the Horseshoe Bar in Drury Street in the city centre.

Inside, behind the ornate detail and immaculately cut lettering on its façade, the Horseshoe Bar has a glorious Victorian interior of stunning opulence: huge gilt mirrors from floor to ceiling, Corinthian columns, ornamental clocks, brass candelabra, a gilt statue of a blacksmith (the site was once a stable), stained glass and, as its centrepiece, a magnificent horseshoe-shaped bar. It's like having a drink in the Palace of Versailles.

Charles Rennie Mackintosh was one of Europe's most
gifted turn-of-the-century architects. His work is generally labelled Art Nouveau although it owes more to
Scottish baronial and vernacular antecedents and a
modern outlook than to the sentiment of the English
Arts and Crafts movement or the decorative, swirling
curves of continental practitioners — Horta in Brussels, Guimard in Paris and Gaudi in Barcelona. You
can even detect a Japanese influence at work inside his
buildings. His interiors often have that cool, meditative quality found in the dark wooden beams and paper
screens of old Japanese houses. This rich source of reference from which Mackintosh drew, allied with his
intuitive talent for composition and fastidious craftsmanship, released him from the architectural straight-
jacket of the time and imbued his work with the idiosyncratic, modern qualities admired today.

Mackintosh was only a draughtsman when he
worked on the Herald building, built in Mitchell Street
in 1893-95. It is one of the earliest works now attributed
to him. A lesser designer might have made it look like
its neighbour, built in 1905, but Mackintosh's pen
moved with an eccentric, Art Nouveau flourish. The
deep shadowed eaves overhang the stylised stonework
on the water tower and the fortress-like massing of the
façade show the Art Nouveau-cum-Scottish Baronial
elements which were to become the hallmarks of his
style. Gordon Chambers next door, imposing though it
is, looks pompous and plodding in comparison, its over-
weight baroque an architectural Watson to Mackintosh's erudite, eccentric Holmes.

80

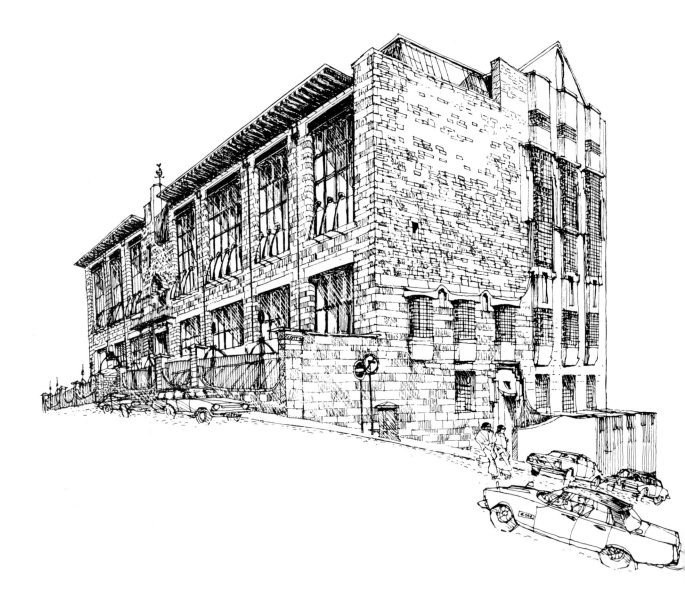

This is the building which put Glasgow on the international architectural map — the Glasgow School of Art. Designed by Charles Rennie Mackintosh, built in two stages, 1897-99 and 1907-09, it is the best known and finest of the few buildings in the city which this Glasgow architect designed. Sadly much of his work never left the drawing board. Looking at the Art School you can see why. This building is so different from the architectural norm of the time that the architectural establishment, never mind potential clients, tended to dismiss Mackintosh with a bluster of complacency and ignorance. This attitude pursued him throughout his career and he eventually left Glasgow for disillusioned exile in England and, subsequently, in the South of France.

Glasgow should be grateful that in Francis Newbery, the Art School's Director, Mackintosh found an enlightened patron who championed the selection of Mackintosh's brave design after an architectural competition. It is a building of world renown and ranks Glasgow with Paris, Vienna, Chicago, Brussels and Barcelona as one of the centres of early 20th-century architecture and design. Mackintosh was a 'pioneer of the Modern Movement'. He challenged the architectural fogeys of the time and sensed a future of innovation in architecture, an artistic response to changing times, as opposed to the regressive sentiment for pompous, past styles with which the late-Victorians embellished their works.

The Glasgow School of Art is a complex and beautiful building. It rewards repeated attention constantly revealing details which, somehow, you never noticed before. This is a building which you have to explore. Such is the Art School's fame that it has an almost arcane status in the modern architectural world — a place of pilgrimage on its hill top. Visitors must be surprised to find it still populated by students who inhabit its labyrinth like a tribe in a temple in the jungle.

Mackintosh was a magician with light and space, height and depth. The interior is a warren of passages and sudden, daylit spaces like clearings in a forest. Huge, white, luminous studios contrast with the troglodyte world of the basement, appropriately, the sculpture department. The precipitous southward panorama over the city from the top floor contrasts with the dark plunge of the stairways, the effect you get when descending from the battlements of an old Scottish tower house. There is a medieval quality to the Art School for all its modern, avant-garde effects which imbues the building with a peculiar resonance. There is a sense of times past as much as there is of the present and future. Mackintosh's genius was to give the building this stimulating personality.

The building's tour-de-force is the library whose iron-framed oriel windows shoot up the wall like skyscrapers. Inside there is a stunning interior of great tranquillity. Its wooden beams, pillars and gallery arranged around a two storey, square space creak as you walk around rather like pine trees swaying softly in a northern forest — the inspiration, it has been suggested, for this superb design.

Outside, in Renfrew Street, the main façade shows Mackintosh's capacity to produce a bold, modern design in harmony with his penchant for idiosyncratic decoration. The asymmetrical composition of huge studio windows is given scale and presence by the delicacy and refinement of his ironwork and by the Art Nouveau detail around the doorway. Mackintosh's ability and originality were unrivalled (and unrecognised) at the time in Glasgow. The Art School building was underrated in Britain at the time and received scant attention from the architectural press. Today, you can't open a book on the architecture of the 20th-century without finding the Art School given its deserved pride of place.

Mackintosh not only designed avant-garde buildings, but complete interiors as well. Every room and corridor in the Art School is marked by his touch as are the exterior and interior of Willow Tearooms in Sauchiehall Street. Mackintosh designed a remarkable series of tearooms in the city for proprietor Kate Cranston. Only at the Willow, however, was he responsible for every aspect of the building (he designed the interiors for the others within existing façades) and it is fitting that it is the Willow which has survived and been restored.

Furniture, fittings, menu-cards and even the cutlery — Mackintosh designed them all. The interior, divided by balconies and openwork screens, demonstrates Mackintosh's intuitive use of space, his feeling for intimacy as well as general effect and magical decorative style. Above the ground floor (now a shop) the *Salon de Luxe* has been reinstated as a tearoom. The furniture here is a reproduction but the fittings are original including the leaded, mirror-glass doors and the similarly treated window which boldly bows across the façade allowing a wave of diffused daylight to illuminate and slide in reflections around the room.

Outside, the clean, modern façade leaps out from the Victorian buildings which flank it. More Vienna Secession than Victorian/Edwardian Glasgow, it gives Sauchiehall Street a flavour of continental bohemia playfully at odds with the tearoom's bourgeois respectability. Mackintosh was, in fact, widely admired on the continent, particularly in Vienna where Josef Hoffmann and other Modernists acknowledged his originality and influence.

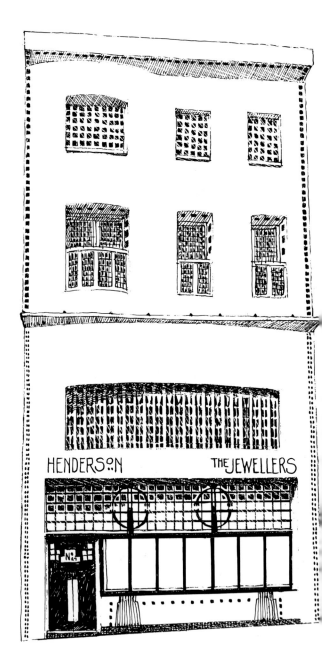

Mackintosh's pioneering modern work did influence some Glasgow architects and interior designers. Collectively he, and they, established a recognisable 'Glasgow Style' as it has come to be called. City firms like Wylie and Lochead produced furniture, fireplaces, stained glass and tile panels in Art Nouveau 'Glasgow Style'. Much of this *fin-de-siècle* bric-a-brac can still be discovered all over the West of Scotland. Many Glasgow tenement closes, for example, are decorated with Art Nouveau tiles. There are even a few Art Nouveau tenements like the Savings Bank at Anderston, designed by James Salmon. Salmon also designed the amazing 'Hatrack' in St Vincent Street.

Known as the 'Hatrack' because of its narrow façade and hooked mullions and dormers it is an original interpretation of the Art Nouveau style. While less florid and sinuous than contemporaries in Paris, Brussels or Barcelona it does give the impression, in common with other Art Nouveau buildings, of having grown up out of the ground rather than having just been plonked down on it. Despite the awkward site (only 10 yards wide) the 'Hatrack's' highly glazed façade allows daylight to penetrate deep inside. Lit up at night, it appears weightless like a huge lantern.

ROBERTA BUCHAN

ROBERTA BUCHAN

THE LION CHAMBERS

VICE CONSOLATO D'ITALIA

BATH LANE

G.A. DOUGLAS STATIONERS

STATIONERS PRINTERS

CO OP

The remarkable Lion Chambers, at the top of Hope Street, was also designed by James Salmon. It was built in 1905 but retains only a hint of Art Nouveau — the style's popularity had begun to wane by that time. There is, however, a strong sense of something modern happening here: the spare, almost abstract quality of the façade; the bravura treatment of the 'wall of glass' on the lane elevation (the lanes sub-dividing Glasgow's city centre blocks often spring this sort of surprise) and the powerful vertical emphasis. There's a skyscraper feel to Lion Chambers although the building only rises eight storeys.

This building is certainly modern in its use of materials. It's not built in stone but in reinforced concrete. The walls are only four inches thick. This was an advanced building for its time, demonstrating the structural freedom which concrete could achieve and hinting at that material's still under-used potential to produce subtly shaped effects of *chiaroscuro* as opposed to squared-off blocks.

BANK OF SCOTLAND

BANK OF SCOTLAN
ST VINCENT STREET

BANK OF SCOTLAN
RENFIELD STREET

By the turn-of-the-century the use of iron, steel and concrete had begun to demonstrate structural possibilities beyond the scope of traditional stone buildings. The steel frame (and the invention of the elevator) allowed buildings of greater height to be built as office blocks in Chicago at the time had shown. Architects in the early 20th century were faced with the problem of how to decorate these new structures where stonework had become structurally superfluous. Those who saw the aesthetic logic in letting the purity and beauty of the structure speak for itself ridiculed the idea of concealing a modern steel building in a cocoon of ornamental stonework. Revolutionary social and industrial changes, the collapse of the *anciens régimes* of 19th-century Europe after the First World War and a general artistic rebellion against Victorian ornamentalism pointed architecture in this modern direction. But traditional taste had a long twilight.

The 1920s saw a flourish of decoration and nostalgia in the neoclassical style favoured by banks, governments and railway companies, particularly in North America. It was a decorative cladding applied to steel frame buildings before the general acceptance of the Modernist 'form follows function' machine aesthetic of steel, concrete and glass. Glasgow has quite a few examples of these American style 1920s office blocks which combine with the grid-plan streets to give parts of central Glasgow a distinctly American urban flavour. One of the most impressive is the Bank of Scotland at the corner of Renfield and St Vincent Streets.

The Bank of Scotland is a monumental structure of Ionic columns and pilasters, topped with a cornice so heavy you wouldn't think the building could support it. The walls of this financial fortress look four feet thick. They're not. They don't even hold the building up. Inside there is a modern steel frame. All the Greek stonework is for show. And yet, there is a solid grandeur about this building. It seems visually positive about its function. You feel your savings would be secure here.

Few architectural styles speak more vividly of their time than the Art Deco of the 1920s and 1930s. Although it flourished in America and is indelibly associated with New York skyscrapers and Hollywood cinemas it derives from the *Exposition des Arts Décoratifs* held in Paris in 1925. This influential exhibition promoted a flamboyant, decorative style which was applied to architecture much as the Victorians had done but with humour rather than pretension.

Easier to draw than to describe, Art Deco and the 1930s Moderne to which it was later married (and is often confused) was a decadent blend of classical Greek and Egyptian forms, jazz age imagery, Art Nouveau and the angular and latterly streamlined geometry of the machine age. This bizarre *mélange* was enriched in America by the influence of pre-Columbian temples (discovered at the time, like Tutankhamun's tomb which provided the Egyptian influence), Cecil B de Mille, ocean liners and the automobile industry — Glasgow's Beresford Hotel looks like a cross between a car radiator grill and a Hollywood film set.

This amazing building 'Glasgow's first skyscraper hotel' brings a brash, New York touch to Sauchiehall Street. Redolent of flapper-girls and bellhops, black Buicks and trans-Atlantic travellers, it was built for the 1938 Empire Exhibition held in the city's Bellahouston Park and named after its builder and proprietor, cinema owner W Beresford Inglis. Moderne rather than Art Deco, the streamlined façade leaps onto the street with gusto and confidence. It's an extraordinary building to find in Glasgow and an important one — there are only a handful of 1930s buildings in the city of this spectacle and quality. No longer used as a hotel, the Beresford is used by Strathclyde University as a hall of residence.

SAUCHIEHALL STREET

THE BERESFORD HOTEL

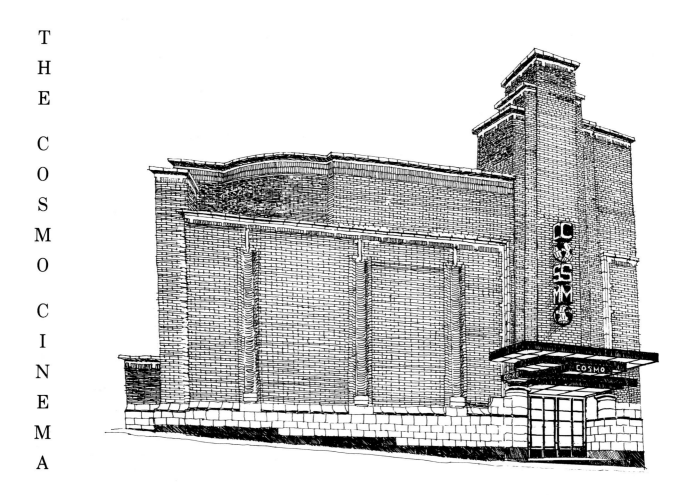

Glasgow once had over 130 cinémas. It was 'Cinema City' with more picture houses per head of population than anywhere outside America. Some early cinemas were richly embellished with interior décor borrowed from the Victorian and Edwardian music halls which they replaced. The Pavilion in Hope Street, a confection of engaging decorative frivolity, is a rare survivor from these music hall days. Many early cinemas were converted theatres but by the 1930s a distinctive cinema style, Hollywood Deco, had begun to appear. A number of cinemas were built in the style in Glasgow during this period. They had streamlined façades outlined at night by neon light and fanciful names — Cosmo, Roxy, Paramount, Toledo — evoking the dream world projected on their silver screens.

The most attractive, if least characteristic, Glasgow picture palace of the 1930s is the former Cosmo in Rose Street. This small cinema was built in 1939 and traditionally specialised in foreign films. This cosmopolitan programming was complemented by the building's architectural style which refers as much to Dutch Expressionist brickwork of the 1920s as it does to the Hollywood Deco/Moderne of the 1930s. The Cosmo is still used as an 'art house' cinema. It is now the Glasgow Film Theatre, a transfer of ownership which, while it may have saved the building, saw the elimination of the Cosmo identity, the removal of the Cosmo globe sign and marquee (which I liked so much I've drawn them back in) and the loss of an elegant Deco foyer. Only a few 1930s cinemas survive in Glasgow and even fewer in anything approaching their original condition. Those which do are now bingo halls, a change of use which, unlike the multi-screen conversions of the 1960s, has not required too much alteration to their architectural character. The former Odeon at Anniesland, for example, opened in 1939, still looks like a picture palace from Hollywood's heyday.

The clean lines and restricted, usually cream, red and black palette of the 1930s Moderne style (as opposed to the decorative disorder and limited poten-tial of Art Deco) gave modern architecture a popular appeal that it has since, unfortunately but under-standably, lost. These 1930s buildings, especially cin-emas where the imagery and romance of film influe-nced popular tase, seemed the epitomy of style and progress. While they were much too meretricious to gain the approval of true Modernists they did much to pro-mote the appreciation and acceptance of the una-dorned, functional beauty which modern architec-ture, at its best, can create.

It would have seemed inconceivable until recently that the cinema architecture of the 1930s would be appreciated, let alone become fashionable once more. But architectural taste has always moved in cycles. Buildings, if they survive long enough, inevitably acquire a patina of time which renders even the most nondescript apparently valuable. This has certainly happened with Victorian buildings which in Glasgow are of an exceptionally high standard. It is now happening with the city's far less numerous 1930s buildings and it is quite likely that some post-war modern architecture in the city will come to be re-assessed.

Increasingly there are exceptions but too few modern buildings have come to terms with Glasgow's urban scale or reflect its architectural traditions. Those which do not attempt to do so conspicuously lack the individual qualities of elegance, proportion and originality by which they might stand aloof and memorable. The superb, sensitive design of the Burrell Collection building does succeed in this respect as does the Glasgow College of Building and Printing.

This 1964 Le Corbusier inspired tower is a direct copy of an un-built skyscraper design by that doyen of Modernism. For this reason alone it is worth some attention. This building, raised above George Square, achieves a real presence and a functional elegance, the result of clear, logical draughtsmanship. It boldly displays its internal structure, an attribute not out of place in view of its function, while the overall composition and see-through glazing gives it an effect of balanced, yet delicate solidity on a precarious hillside site. There's even a playful, unexpected artistry in the Le Corbusier style service units on the roof. They look like primitive sculptures, arcane and mysteriously significant. They hint at lost or future civilisations.

Few modern buildings are imbued with such qualities of imagination or elegance. The failed Utopian planning schemes and the uninspired, shoddy office blocks which litter our cities will not be reassessed with any great sympathy. Nor do they deserve to be. There

is a danger, though, that the virtues of some modern buildings may be ignored since modern architecture is currently viewed with general distaste and the mistakes of the recent past have sapped confidence in its ability to provide a livable environment. Turning away from our own time, producing sub-Victorian or Art Deco, post-Modern frippery, is not positive. In Glasgow the strength and quality of Victorian buildings make any imitation, short of a straight copy (a good idea in the case of tenements) look second-rate. The city's Victorian buildings are so good of their type that they can stand, indeed would gain, outwith conservation areas, by being juxtaposed with modern buildings of real quality were these to be built. For the moment, however, the stone-cleaned Victorian buildings stand as symbols of Glasgow's renaissance. They are reminders of a time when it was a great city and support the claim that it still is. Glasgow's rich heritage of Victorian architecture demands, by comparison, that the modern, revitalised city being built around it should aspire to its spirit and quality as I hope this book has shown.

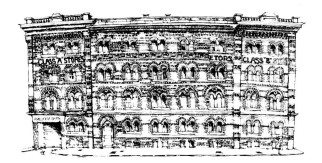

Kingston Grain Mills

Robin Ward was born in Glasgow in 1950. He was brought up and educated in the city, his early years being spent in a tenement house near St George's Cross. After leaving school in 1969 he emigrated to Canada where he worked for the Hudson's Bay Company fur trading with Red Indians and for a mining company working underground in the wilds of northern Manitoba. His varied career has also included labouring for the Forestry Commission in the Scottish West Highlands, working as a traffic officer at Glasgow Airport and as a graphic designer with the BBC (where he met his Thai wife). He returned from Canada in 1972 and studied for four years at the Glasgow School of Art. On completing his course in graphic design, photography and illustration he was awarded a travelling scholarship to Europe. He has since visited many cities in Europe, North America and the Far East but, admits, is inexorably pulled back to his home town. During his time at art school he wrote and illustrated articles for the *Glasgow Herald* on the city's then vanishing Victorian architecture, alerting Glaswegians to the incomparable façades above the city's shopfronts. Robin Ward's other books include *The Spirit of Glasgow,* a collection of his photographs of the city, also published by Richard Drew.